EVEN THE STARS LOOK LONESOME

BANTAM BOOKS BY MAYA ANGELOU

Ask your bookseller for those that you have missed

I Know Why the Caged Bird Sings

Gather Together in My Name

Singin' and Swingin' and Gettin' Merry Like Christmas

The Heart of a Woman

Maya Angelou: Poems

I Shall Not Be Moved

Wouldn't Take Nothing for My Journey Now

Even the Stars Look Lonesome

Maya Angelou

EVEN THE STARS LOOK LONESOME

BANTAM BOOKS
NEW YORK TORONTO LONDON SYDNEY AUCKLAND

EVEN THE STARS LOOK LONESOME

A Bantam Book / Published by arrangement with
Random House, Inc.

PUBLISHING HISTORY
Random House edition published September 1997
Bantam trade edition / September 1998

Many of these essays have been previously published in different form.
Grateful acknowledgment is made to the following for permission to reprint previously
published material:

BOA Editions Limited: "miss rosie" from *Good Woman: Poems and a Memoir 1969–1980* by
Lucille Clifton. Copyright © 1987 by Lucille Clifton. Reprinted by permission of BOA
Editions Limited, Rochester, NY 14604.

Thompson and Thompson: Excerpt of 10 lines from "Heritage" from *Colors* by Countee
Cullen. Copyrights held by the Amistad Research Center, administered by Thompson and
Thompson, New York, NY. Reprinted by permission of Thompson and Thompson.

Alfred A. Knopf, Inc., and Harold Ober Associates, Inc.: "Minstrel Man" from *Collected Poems* by
Langston Hughes. Copyright © 1994 by the Estate of Langston Hughes. Rights throughout
the British Commonwealth are controlled by Harold Ober Associates, Inc. Reprinted by
permission of Alfred A. Knopf, Inc., and Harold Ober Associates, Inc.

MCA Music Publishing: Excerpt from "Key to the Highway," words and music by Big Bill
Broonzy and Chas. Segar. Copyright © 1941, 1963 by MCA-DUCHESS MUSIC
CORPORATION. Copyright renewed by MCA-DUCHESS MUSIC
CORPORATION. International copyright secured. All rights reserved. Reprinted by
permission of MCA Music Publishing.

Reed Visuals: Excerpt from "I Am a Black Woman" from *I Am a Black Woman* by Mari
Evans (New York: William Morrow & Company, 1970).
Copyright © 1970 by Mari Evans. Reprinted by permission of the author.

University Press of Virginia: "Little Brown Baby" from *The Collected Poetry of Paul Laurence
Dunbar* edited by Joanne Braxton, published in 1993. Copyright © 1993. Reprinted by
permission of University Press of Virginia.

BOOK DESIGN BY CAROLE LOWENSTEIN

Library of Congress Catalog Card Number: 97-17317

ISBN: 0-553-37972-0

Published simultaneously in the United States and Canada

Bantam Books are published by Bantam Books, a division of Bantam
Doubleday Dell Publishing Group Inc. Its trademark, consisting of the
words "Bantam Books" and the portrayal of a rooster, is Registered in U.S.
Patent and Trademark Office and in other countries. Marca Registrada.
Bantam Books, 1540 Broadway, New York, New York 10036.

PRINTED IN THE UNITED STATES OF AMERICA
QMB   10   9   8   7   6   5   4   3   2   1

These thoughts are dedicated to the children who will come to maturity in the twenty-first century.

Their charge will be to eliminate warfare, promote equality, exile disease, establish justice and increase joy. In fact, to make this a perfect world. A partial listing of those I know and love includes:

Elliott Jones
Latasha Payne Johnson
Dori Colly
Shannon Fulcher
Asia Simpson
Stevie Jones Sharpe
Brianna Elizabeth Lear
Madeline Rose Lear
Tabari Mabon
Devyn LaCamera
Anthony Fulcher
Miles Loomis
Danté Glenn
Naima Muhammad
Travis Thompson
Monique Kelley
Ashley McPherson
Andrea McPherson

Devin Williams
Alandra Hawkins
Jurel Hawkins
Kenya Christina Garris
Christopher Johnson
Patrick Johnson
Talisha Potts
Christopher MacRae
Sean MacRae
Mark MacRae
Akeem Jamal Johnson
George Two Rogers
The Shestack Children
Benjamin Lear
Jasmin Andrews
Jackie Robert Kelley, Jr.
Danielle McPherson

AND ALL THE CHILDREN OF THE WORLD

Contents

A House
Can Hurt,
a Home
Can Heal

My last marriage was made in heaven. The musical accompaniment was provided by Gabriel, and angels were so happy that ten thousand of them danced on the head of a pin. It was the marriage to end all my marriages. My husband had dropped out of architecture school and become a builder. In fact, in Britain, where he had lived, he was called a master builder. We married in Los Angeles, where he bought and rebuilt old houses, then sold them at handsome profits. We then moved to Sonoma County, where he found more old houses to refurbish. He restored a genteel, polished look to old Victorians and modernized 1930s bungalows. After several years of rapturous married life we moved to the Pacific Palisades, into a futuristic condo that thrust its living room out over a California canyon with a daring and an insouciance usually to be found only in a practiced drunk pretending sobriety. There in that very expensive and posh settlement the foundation of my marriage began to collapse.

With all heart-sore lovers I say, "I don't know

what went wrong." But I suspect it was the house. The living room was two stories high, and I put my large three-by-five-foot paintings on the walls, and upon those vast reaches they diminished and began to look little better than enlarged color posters. I laid my Indian and Pakistani rugs on the floor over the beige wall-to-wall carpeting and they drowned in the vastness of the living room, appearing little more than colorful table mats on a large boardroom table.

Everything was built in—standard oven, microwave oven, grill, garbage disposal, compactor. There was nothing for my husband to do.

Before, when our marriage had shown weakness—as all marriages do, I suppose—I would argue with my husband on his procrastination in taking out the garbage or his failure to separate the cans from the glass bottles, or his refusal to brush the Weber clean and empty the ashes. But, alas, since the house did everything itself, I couldn't blame him for his inconsequential failures, and was forced to face up to our real problems.

Floundering or not, we still had the ability to talk to each other. I asked what he thought was the matter, and he said, "It's this damned house. We are simple people and it is too damned pretentious." (I did question if we were truly simple people. I was the first black female writer/producer at Twentieth

Century-Fox, a member of the board of trustees of the American Film Institute, and a lecturer at universities around the world—from Yale to the university in Milan, Italy. He was a builder from London, a graduate of the London School of Economics, the first near-nude centerfold for *Cosmopolitan* magazine, and formerly the husband of Germaine Greer. Our credentials, good and bad, hardly added up to our being simple people.)

We agreed that the house was separating us. He thought it was time to move back to northern California, where the grass was greener and the air purer, and we could live simpler lives. I would write poetry and he would build ordinary houses.

He went on a quest to the Bay Area and found an Art Deco house in the hills of Oakland with a magnificent view of the Golden Gate Bridge. His happiness was contagious. Our marriage was back on track. We were a rather eccentric, loving, unusual couple determined to live life with flair and laughter. We bought the house on Castle Drive from a couple who had married a year before and had been busy bringing the house back to its original classical three pastel colors. I admit, it was a little disconcerting to find that the couple had divorced before they even moved into the house. But I decided that that was their affair and was not necessarily a bad omen for our new house.

My husband and I moved in. The beautiful parquet floors welcomed my Oriental rugs. In hanging my paintings I had to adjust to some of the round corners, but I adjusted. My oversized sofas were primed to offer comfort to those who wanted to sit and look out over the garden and at the bay. There was a room that was a bar, and its circular windows opened into the kitchen, where there was no compactor, no garbage disposal, one oven and a gas range. The piano sat in one corner of the spacious living room, and we set up handsome card tables in the bar so that we could entertain ourselves and our guests at bid whist and other parlor games. I thought, Now, this is the way to live.

Within a month I realized the house hated me. It was no consolation that it hated my husband as well. I was known as a good cook, and sometimes there were even flashes of brilliance in my culinary efforts. But in that house on Castle Drive, if I made bread or cakes they would inevitably fall into soggy, resentful masses. When I fried chicken, the skin and batter would be crisp and at the bone there would be blood as red as cherries. The king-sized bed we had brought from Berkeley to Los Angeles and back to Oakland fell in the middle of the night without any prompting of activity by the occupants. My drapes, hung by professionals, came off the runners. The doors began not to fit the frame, and my piano would not stay in tune. The house hated us.

My Airedale, Toots, preferred to stay out in the yard in the cold rather than enter the house. We had the bother and the expense of building a doghouse, although the dog had been intended to be house company for me. Within six months my husband and I were hardly speaking to each other, and within a year of moving into that formal architectural edifice we agreed to call a halt to the struggle to save our marriage.

We owned two large houses. I went away for three weeks, asking that when I returned he would be moved into one of them taking whatever he wanted of the furniture, paintings, linens and other things we had accumulated together.

I returned to the house on a dark evening and was reminded of something I had said to an interviewer years earlier. I had been asked what I would like as my last meal if I was going to die. I had replied, "I don't want to think that far ahead, but if I were going to Mars tomorrow I would like to have hot chicken, a chilled bottle of white wine and a loaf of good bread." When I went into the darkened house, I was greeted by the aroma of roast chicken. There was a note on the refrigerator that read, "There is a hot chicken in the oven, a cold bottle of wine in the fridge and a loaf of good bread on the cutting board. Thank you for the good times." Now, that's the kind of man I wanted to marry and did marry. And if it wasn't for those two damned bad houses, I would still be married to him.

My husband announced that he was going to stay in the Bay Area. I decided that since we had jointly found the best restaurants, the best friends, the best bars, the best parks, it was inevitable that if I stayed there that I would walk into a restaurant one day or into a bar one night and he would be there with my new replacement, or he would walk into a restaurant or a bar one evening and I would be sitting there with his replacement. Our relationship had been too friendly to allow us to risk that sort of embarrassment. So I gave my ex-husband the Bay Area—I gave him San Francisco and Oakland and the hills and the bays and the bridges, and all that beauty. And I moved to North Carolina. I thought I'd find a small, neat little bungalow and I'd step into it and pull its beautiful walls around my shoulders. I thought that was very poetic, and that way I would just sort of muddle through the rest of my life.

However, once I got to North Carolina, I realized that my gigantic old-fashioned furniture would not be accommodated in a bungalow. I also considered that if I moved from a ten-room house in the hills of Oakland to anything smaller, I would be implying, at least to myself, that my circumstances had been reduced. So I started looking for a large house, and I found one.

When I walked into it, the woman who was selling it had the good sense and the wit to be baking gingersnap cookies and fresh bread. The place reeked of home. The aroma reached out to the landing, put its arms around me and walked me through the front door.

I offered a large sum of money in good faith and explained that I wanted to lease the house for a year, and if I didn't buy the house after that time I would forfeit the good-faith money. The owners said I didn't need to do that. They had read my work and said they wanted me to have the house, and offered me terms that I found impossible to refuse.

I bought the house, and as I refurbished it, it also molded me. I added a bedroom for my grandson, who had been missing for four years. He was returned as the room was completed. A man whom I had adored from a distance declared his undying love for me.

When I took the house it had ten rooms, and I have added on more. At present it has eighteen rooms. My builder asked me if I was thinking of reaching the next street down from my house. This is no longer my house, it is my home. And because it is my home, I have not only found myself healed of the pain of a broken love affair, but discovered that when something I have written does not turn out as I had hoped, I am not hurt so badly. I find that my physical ailments, which are a part of growing older, do not depress me so deeply. I find that I am quicker to laugh and much quicker to forgive. I am much happier at receiving small gifts and more delighted to be a donor of large gifts. And all of that because I am settled in my home.

My life and good fortune carry me around the world. However, when I am on a plane and the pilot announces, "Ladies and gentlemen, we have begun our descent into North Carolina," my burdens lift, my heart is at ease and a smile finds its way all the way across my face. I know that soon I will be in a car that will stop on a quiet street in Winston-Salem, and I will step out and be home again.

Africa

What is Africa to me?" asks Countee Cullen in his poem "Heritage," written in 1926.

> *What is Africa to me:*
> *Copper sun or scarlet sea,*
> *Jungle star or jungle track,*
> *Strong bronzed men, or regal black*
> *Women from whose loins I sprang*
> *When the birds of Eden sang?*
> *One three centuries removed*
> *From the scenes his fathers loved,*
> *Spicy grove, cinnamon tree,*
> *What is Africa to me?*

Until a few decades ago the answers to that question might well have included anything from the subhuman caterwauling of Tarzan to Ernest Hemingway's depiction of the romantic Dark Continent populated with wild animals, white hunters and black bearers. Many black as well as white Americans were equally ignorant of both African history and African culture.

In the days before "Black is beautiful" was a rallying cry, even before the 1954 Supreme Court decision to ban segregation in public schools, I studied dance in New York with the legendary Pearl Primus. Ms. Primus was a social anthropologist, a famous concert dancer and an exacting teacher. On a research visit to Africa she had been given the name Omowale, "child who has returned home." She came back to the United States with a fierce determination to teach African dance down to the last authentic detail.

After I had studied with her for a year, Ms. Primus, who was not given to even meager compliments, told me that I might, just might, become a good dancer and even a decent teacher. Armed with this gracious commendation, I headed to a Midwestern city that boasted of having a progressive American Negro (the word was acceptable then) cultural center. I was engaged as dance instructor, and lasted two weeks. The black middle-class families whose children were in my class protested in one voice, "Why is she teaching African dance to our children? We haven't lost anything in Africa."

There is one major explanation for the old negative image of Africa and all things African held by so many. Slavery's profiteers had to convince themselves and their clients that the persons they enslaved were little better than beasts. They could not admit that the

Africans lived in communities based upon sociopolitical structures no better or worse than their European counterparts of the time. The slave sellers had to persuade slave buyers that the African was a primitive, a cannibal, and richly deserved oppression. How else could the Christian voice be silent—how soothe the Christian conscience?

African history and culture have been shrouded in centuries of guilt and ignorance and shame. The African slaves themselves, separated from their tribesmen and languages, forced by the lash to speak another tongue immediately, were unable to convey the stories of their own people, their deeds, rituals, religions and beliefs. In the United States the slaves were even exiled from the drums, instruments of instruction, ceremony and entertainment of their homeland. Within a few generations details of the kingdoms of Ghana and Mali and of the Songhai Empire became hazy in their minds. The Mende concept of beauty and the Ashanti idea of justice all but faded with the old family names and intricate tribal laws. The slaves too soon began to believe what their masters believed: Africa was a continent of savages.

Save for the rare scholar and the observant traveler, the African at home (on the continent) was seen as a caricature of nature; so it followed that the Africans abroad (blacks everywhere) were better only because of their encounters with whites. Even in religious matters, the African was called a mere fetishist, trusting in sticks and bones. Most failed to see the correlation between the African and his gris-gris (religious amulets) and the Moslem with his beads or the Catholic with his rosary.

How, then, to explain that these people, supposedly without a culture, could so influence the cultures of their captors and even of distant strangers with whom they have had no contact?

Most social dance around the world, if it is not ethnic—polka, hora or hula—can be seen as having been influenced by African movement. Internationally popular music has been molded by the blues, and shaped by jazz. The Beatles gave honor to Afro-American music as the source of their inspiration, and Elvis Presley particularly thanked the old blues singer Arthur "Big Boy" Crudup for inspiring his beat and style. The Museum of Modern Art has an exhibit showing the remarkable influence of African sculpture upon the art of Picasso, Modigliani and Klee. International style, which includes fashion, speech and humor, would be wan and weak without the infusion of African creativity.

I lived in West Africa for over four years and frequently encountered behavior I had known in the United States that I had thought to be black American in origin or, at the very least, southern American. I found that Africans in a group, whether related by blood or by marriage, were called by familial names: uncle, bubba, brother, tuta, sister, mama, papa, and I knew that American blacks continued that practice. Reluctantly I had to admit that while the characteristics of Uncle Tom and Aunt Jemima were fictional, created in the fantasies of unknowing whites, the appellations Uncle and Auntie had certainly been brought from Africa and planted into the consciousness of the New World by uprooted slaves. Black Americans' attitudes in churches, their call and response and funeral marches are African carryovers, and herbal therapies are still actively practiced that can be traced back to Africa, their place of origin.

Although millions of Africans were taken from the continent from the sixteenth until the middle of the nineteenth century, many Africans on the continent display no concern over the descendants of their lost ancestors. Many have no knowledge that their culture has been spread around the world by those same hapless and sometimes hopeless descendants. African culture is alive and well. An African proverb spells out the truth: "The ax forgets. The tree remembers."

Aging

*I*n the crisp days of my youth whenever I was asked what I thought about growing old, I always responded with a nervous but brassy rejoinder that hid my profound belief that I never expected to live past twenty-eight. Tears would fill my eyes and bathe my face when I thought of dying before my son reached puberty. I was thirty-six before I realized I had lived years beyond my deadline and needed to revise my thinking about an early death. I would live to see my son an adult and myself at the half-century mark. With that realization life waxed sweeter. Old acquaintances became friendships, and new clever acquaintances showed themselves more interesting. Old loves burdened with memories of disappointments and betrayals packed up and left town, leaving no forwarding address, and new loves came calling.

I decided I would consent to living to an old and venerable age. White strands of hair would combine to make a startling snow-white narrow streak emerging near my temple. I would speak more slowly, choosing my words with the deliberation of an elder stateswoman, a Madame de Staël or a Mary McLeod Bethune. I would wear lovely floral scents—lavender and lilac—reminiscent of lace handkerchiefs and old-fashioned sachets. My clothes would gradually become more distinguished-looking: gray suits, with good brooches on the lapels, and elegant dresses. And while I would refuse on pain of death to wear old ladies' comforts, I would give away the three-inch spike heels that had given me the advantage of being taller than nearly everyone else in the world. And I would choose good shoes with medium heels save for the odd gold or silver pumps for black-tie affairs.

Those were my plans. Oh, yes, I would keep company with other old women who would be friends equally dolled-up, and I would always have an elegant dapper man holding my arm.

Those were my plans, but Robert Burns was right: "The best laid schemes . . ." Mine certainly went awfully a-gley.

At sixty my body, which had never displayed a mind of its own, turned obstreperous, opinionated and deliberately treacherous. The skin on my thighs became lumpy, my waist thickened and my breasts— It's better not to mention them at all except to say that they seemed to be in a race to see which could be first to reach my knees.

Doubt and pessimism came to me in a terrible
Siamese-twin embrace:

> *The loss of love and youth*
> *and fire came raiding,*
> *riding,*
> *a horde of plunderers*
> *on one caparisoned steed,*
> *sucking up the sun drops,*
> *trampling the green shoots*
> *of my carefully planted years.*
>
> *The evidence: thickened waist and*
> *leathery thighs, which triumph*
> *over my fallen insouciance.*
>
> *After fifty-five*
> *the arena has changed.*
> *I must enlist new warriors.*
> *My resistance,*
> *once natural as raised voices,*
> *importunes in the dark.*
> *Is this battle worth the candle?*
> *Is this war worth the wage?*
>
> *May I not greet age*
> *without a grouse, allowing*
> *the truly young to own*
> *the stage?*

But now, as I wend nearer to my seventieth year, my optimism has returned.

My appetites have also returned with ravenous lustiness. True, I can't eat *choucroute garnie* or fried chicken with potato salad and then head for bed. I eat smaller portions earlier and try to take a short walk. A smooth scotch still causes me to smile, and a decent wine is received with gratitude. Men and music still bring great delight, of course, sometimes in moderation. Mostly, what I have learned so far about aging, despite the creakiness of one's bones and the cragginess of one's once-silken skin, is this: do it. By all means, do it.

Godfrey
Cambridge
and Fame

Godfrey Cambridge was an out-of-work comedian, an occasionally employed taxi driver and my pal-about-town partner. I would have gladly traded the buddy relationship for a romantic affair with him, but, like so many men, Godfrey was interested only in women who were not interested in him. I have not decided whether that attitude stemmed from delight in the chase or a kind of masochism.

In the fifties I made a reasonable living for myself and my son as a nightclub singer. When I signed a contract to perform at the Gate of Horn in Chicago, friends in New York gave a celebratory party for me. Godfrey offered to pick me up in his taxi and drop me off. He promised to come back around two, spend a few minutes and take me to my home in Brooklyn.

After enjoying the dance floor for nearly an hour, I moved toward a seat, but not without looking around for my audience. A part of the pleasure of dancing derived from knowing that even some professionals liked to see me dance. I liked their liking me and I never resisted the urge to catch the admiration on their faces, in their eyes.

That night I was dumbfounded. To my astonishment no one was looking at me. Every eye was focused on a whale of a man who sat in Buddha-like repose against a far wall. A few people gingerly approached the huge figure while those who only dared to watch him timorously sat or stood away in rapt attention.

I was not a true New Yorker, and possibly neither were the others present, but at least they had seniority, and while I had no idea who the man was, I certainly would not have called my ignorance to anyone's attention.

I found my way to the bar and engaged the unrapt bartender in conversation. After two drinks I decided not to give up on my unfaithful admirers. I began to search out partners to dance with me. Finding no one, I danced alone, whirling and twirling to my own delight until I tired myself out.

After another visit to the bar, I crossed the cleared area that was used as a dance floor to approach the man mountain who I had secretly decided was a drug kingpin. His voice was part growl, part whisper: "Hey. What's your name?"

I said, "Maya. What's yours?"

He said, "Myra? What you doing here? Who you come with?"

I drew all my height, my youth, my training into an obelisk of dignity. "This party was given for me. May I ask what *you* are doing here?"

His voice was a perfect match for his bulk. "Buddy Young brought me and we're getting ready to go. This your birthday or something?"

I knew he wouldn't understand, but I told him anyway. "This is a bon voyage party. I'm leaving to-morrow for Chicago. I am a singer."

"I want to call you. Myra, I like the way you dance. Where do you stay in Chicago? I'm going to be wrestling over there."

Hmm, at least he had noticed my choreodrama. I told him the name of the hotel.

He asked, "And your name is Myra? What's the rest?"

I told him. He said, "I'm going to call you. Eugene Lipscomb. Don't forget me. I'm Eugene Lipscomb."

He pushed past me.

Godfrey returned and was running late, so when he came to get me, he had both our coats. "Let's go. I can still get a couple of hours before daybreak."

We said our good-byes.

As we neared his parked taxi, he asked, "Some-body said you had been talking to some big dude. Who was it? Are you planning to see him later?"

I said, "Hardly. He couldn't figure out how to pro-nounce my name. Kept calling me Myra." I began to

mimic the big man. "Myra, don't forget I'm Eugene—Eugene Lipscomb."

Godfrey stopped, gasped and grabbed my shoulders, all at once.

"Did you say Eugene Lipscomb?"

I nodded my head. He was shaking me.

"Girl, don't you know who he is? Don't you
know that's Big Daddy Lipscomb, the greatest tackle
in the world? The star of the Green Bay Packers?"

He let me go and, turning around, ran on the icy
sidewalk as if he himself were one of the Green Bay
Packers and he was trying to duck around Big Daddy.

I was left alone in the bitter-cold early morning air
while my buddy went back into the warm apartment
to grovel at the feet of a man who had already left and
whom I deemed unworthy of my serious notice.

I'm wrong—I was not left alone. I had for company embarrassment and remorse over my supercil-
ious behavior. I was also left with a lesson that
unfortunately I was to learn again and again.

If a little learning is dangerous, a little fame can be
devastating. The wise woman thinks twice and speaks
once or, better yet, does not speak at all. Keeps her silence, her thoughts and her equilibrium appearing to
be knowledgeable even when she is not, and, above
all, does not allow a little celebrity to convince her
that just because she is capable of reading the name of

the approaching station, she should not believe that she has arrived.

On some public occasions, I have acted wisely, sagely with studied poise and control. At other times I have behaved with less subtlety than a Neanderthal rooting for his supper.

How does fame or celebrity affect our encounters with others?

There is a moment I dread, for I'm not always sure in advance of how I will behave. For example, a stranger approaches and says to me, "I've noticed that everyone at this party [or on this plane or in this restaurant] seems to know you. Well, I don't. Are you anybody?" At such times, I may smile and answer enigmatically, "Thank you so much." Or I may say, "Probably not. If you, who are somebody, have to ask." And at my worst I have said, "Yes. I am a poet. And a very famous one at that, and I am sorry you didn't know it." As soon as that piece of arrogance has left my mouth, I shrivel up. I begin to wonder if I am so inflated by the Creator's gift that God might become irritated and take it from me.

The African saying is "The trouble for the thief is not how to steal the chief's bugle, but where to blow it." I translate that to signify, the trouble for the receiver is not just how to accept a gift (even the gift of fame) but with what grace the recipient shares it.

A Song to Sensuality

*T*here is a cruel and stupid intolerance among the young. I know that is so because at the tender age of thirty I was given to declaim in injured tones: "Old women of fifty look awful in ropes of colored beads, thong sandals and fresh flowers in their hair" and "I've had it with old men [of fifty also] whose skin has gone to leather yet still wear open-neck shirts and heavy gold chains down to their crotches." I was not always careful whether or not the object of my derision could overhear me because I thought that if I spoke loudly maybe the old person would be lucky enough to learn something about proper dressing. Ah hah.

Ah hah, indeed. Now that I am firmly settled into my fifth decade, and pressing resolutely toward my sixth, I find nothing pleases me so much as gaudy out-sized earrings, off-the-shoulder blouses and red hibiscus blooms pinned in my hair.

Do I look awful? Possibly to the young. Do I feel awful? Decidedly not. I have reached the lovely age where I can admit that sensuality satisfies me as much as sexuality and sometimes more so. I do not mean to suggest that standing on a hill in San Francisco, being buffeted by a fresh wind as I view the western sun setting into the bay, will give me the same enjoyment as a night of lovemaking with the man of my fantasy. On the other hand, while the quantity of pleasure may weigh more heavily on the side of lovemaking, the quality between the two events is equal.

Leers and lascivious smirks to the contrary, sensuality does not necessarily lead to sex, nor is it meant to be a substitute for sex. Sensuality is its own reward.

There are some who are so frightened by the idea of sensual entertainment that they make even their dwelling places bleak and joyless. And what is horrible is that they would have others share that lonely landscape. Personally, I'll have no part of it. I want all my senses engaged.

I would have my ears filled with the world's music, the grunts of hewers of wood, the cackle of old folks sitting in the last sunlight and the whir of busy bees in the early morning. I want to hear the sharp sound of tap dancing and the mournful murmur of a spiritual half remembered and then half sung. I want the clashing cymbals of a marching band and the whisper of a lover entreating a beloved. Let me hear anxious parents warning their obstreperous offspring and a pedantic pedagogue teaching a bored class the mysteries of thermodynamics. All sounds of life and living, death and dying are welcome to my ears.

My eyes will gladly receive colors; the burnt-orange skin of old black women who ride on buses and the cool lavender of certain people's eyes. I like the tomato-red dresses of summer and the sienna of a highly waxed mahogany table. I love the dark green of rain forests and the sunshine yellow of a bowl of lemons. Let my eager sight rest on the thick black of a starless night and the crisp white of fresh linen. And I will have blue. The very pale blue of some complexions and the bold blue of flags. The iridescent blue of hummingbird wings and the dusty blue of twilight in North Carolina. I am not daunted by the blood-red of birth and the red blood of death. My eyes absorb the world's variety and uniqueness.

Taste and smell are firmly joined in wedded bliss. About the bliss I cannot speak, but I can say much about that marriage. I like it that the fleeting scent of fresh-cut citrus and the flowery aroma of strawberries will make my salivary glands pour into my mouth a warm and pure liquid. I accept the salt of tears evoked by sweet onions and betrayed love. Give me the smell of the sea and the wild scent of mountain pines. I do not spurn the suffocating smell of burned rubber of city streets nor the scent of fresh sweat because their pungency reminds me of the bitterness of chocolate

and the sting of vinegar. Some of life's greatest plea-
sures are conveyed by the dual senses of taste and
smell.

In this tribute to sensuality I have saved the sense
of touch as the last pleasure to be extolled. I wish for
the slick feel of silk underclothes and the pinch of
sand in my beach shoes. I welcome the sun strong on
my back and the tender pelting of snow on my face.
Good clothes that fit snugly without squeezing and
strong fearless hands that caress without pain. I want
the crunch of hazelnuts between my teeth and ice
cream melting on my tongue.

I will have that night of sexuality with the man
who inhabits my fantasy. I'll take the sensuality and
the sexuality. Who made the rule that one must
choose either or?

They Came
to Stay

I
am a black woman
tall as a cypress
strong
beyond all definition still
defying place
and time
and circumstance
assailed
impervious
indestructible
Look
on me and be
*renewed**

Black women whose ancestors were brought to the United States beginning in 1619 have lived through conditions of cruelties so horrible, so bizarre, the

*Mari Evans, *I Am A Black Woman*.

women had to reinvent themselves. They had to find safety and sanctity inside themselves or they would not have been able to tolerate such torture. They had to learn quickly to be self-forgiving, for often their exterior actions were at odds with their interior beliefs. Still they had to survive as wholly and healthily as possible in an infectious and sick climate.

Lives lived in such cauldrons are either obliterated or forged into impenetrable alloys. Thus, early on and consciously, black women became realities only to themselves. To others they were mostly seen and described in the abstract, concrete in their labor but surreal in their humanness.

They knew the burden of feminine sensibilities suffocated by masculine responsibilities.

They wrestled with the inescapable horror of undergoing pregnancies that could only result in feeding more chattels into the rapacious maw of slavery.

They knew the grief of enforced separations from mates who were not theirs to claim, for the men themselves did not have legal possession of their own bodies.

> *And men, whose sole crime was their hue,*
> *the impress of their Maker's hand,*
> *and frail and shrinking children too*
> *were gathered in that mournful band**

*Frances Ellen Watkins Harper, *The Slave Auction.*

The larger society, observing the women's outrageous persistence in holding on, staying alive, thought it had no choice but to translate the perversity and contradictions of the black woman's life into a fabulous fiction of multiple personalities. They were seen as acquiescent, submissive Aunt Jemimas with grinning faces, plump laps, fat embracing arms and brown jaws pouched in laughter. They were described as leering buxom wenches with round heels, open thighs and insatiable sexual appetites. They were accused of being marauding matriarchs of stern demeanor, battering hands, unforgiving gazes and castrating behavior.

When we imagine women inhabited by all these apparitions, it becomes obvious that such perceptions were national, racial and historical hallucinations. The contradictions stump even the most fertile imagination, for they could not have existed without the romantic racism that introduced them into the American psyche. Surprisingly, above all, many women did survive as themselves. We meet them, undeniably strong, unapologetically direct.

This is not to sing the praises of the black woman's stamina. Rather, it is a salute to her as an outstanding representative of the human race. Kudos to the educators, athletes, dancers, judges, janitors, politicians, artists, actors, writers, singers, poets and social activists, to all who dare to look at life with humor, determination and respect. They do not abide hypocrisy and those who would practice chicanery find the honesty of these women terrifying.

The heartbreaking tenderness of black women and their majestic strength speak of the heroic survival of a people who were stolen into subjugation, denied chastity and refused innocence.

These women have descended from grandmothers and great-grandmothers who knew the lash firsthand, and to whom protection was nothing more than an abstraction. Their faces are here for the ages to regard and wonder, but they are whole women. Their hands have brought new life into the world, nursed the sick and folded the winding-sheets. Their wombs have held the promise of a race that has proved in each challenging century that despite threats and mayhem it has come to stay. Their feet have trod the shifting swampland of insecurity, yet they have tried to step neatly onto the footprints of mothers who went before. They are not apparitions; they are not superwomen; despite the enormity of their struggles they are not larger than life. Their humanness is evident in their accessibility. We are able to enter into the spirit of these women and rejoice in their warmth and courage.

Precious jewels all. Thanks to their persistence, art, sublime laughter and love we may all yet survive our grotesque history.

Mother and
Freedom

She stood before me, a dolled-up, pretty yellow woman, seven inches shorter than my six-foot bony frame. Her eyes were soft and her voice was brittle. "You're determined to leave? Your mind's made up?"

I was seventeen and burning with passionate rebelliousness. I was also her daughter, so whatever independent spirit I had inherited had been nurtured by living with her and observing her for the past four years.

"You're leaving my house?"

I collected myself inside myself and answered, "Yes. Yes, I've found a room."

"And you're taking the baby?"

"Yes."

She gave me a smile, half proud and half pitying.

"All right, you're a woman. You don't have a husband, but you've got a three-month-old baby. I just want you to remember one thing. From the moment you leave this house, don't let anybody raise you. Every time you get into a relationship you will have to make concessions, compromises, and there's nothing wrong with that. But keep in mind Grandmother Henderson in Arkansas and I have given you every law you need to live by. Follow what's right. You've been raised."

More than forty years have passed since Vivian Baxter liberated me and handed me over to life. During those years I have loved and lost, I have raised my son, set up a few households and walked away from many. I have taken life as my mother gave it to me on that strange graduation day all those decades ago.

In the intervening time when I have extended myself beyond my reach and come toppling Humpty-Dumpty-down on my face in full view of a scornful world, I have returned to my mother to be liberated by her one more time. To be reminded by her that although I had to compromise with life, even life had no right to beat me to the ground, to batter my teeth down my throat, to make me knuckle down and call it Uncle. My mother raised me, and then freed me.

And now, after so many eventful years of trials, successes and failures, my attention is drawn to a bedroom adjoining mine where my once feisty mother lies hooked by pale blue wires to an oxygen tank, fighting cancer for her life.

I think of Vivian Baxter, and I remember Frederick Douglass's mother, enslaved on a plantation eleven miles from her infant son, yet who, after toiling a full day, would walk the distance to look at her child hoping that he would sense a mother's love, then return to the plantation in time to begin another day of labor. She believed that a mother's love brought freedom. Many African Americans know that the most moving song created during the centuries of slavery was and remains "Sometimes I Feel Like a Motherless Child."

As a mother and a daughter myself, I have chosen certain songs and poems to take to my mother's room, and there we will laugh and cry together.

I pray I shall have the courage to liberate my mother when the time comes. She would expect that from me.

Loving
Learning

*T*here are smart alecks who feel comfortable speaking long and loudly about a multiplicity of subjects with no evidence that they know what they are talking about. Then there are those who do know a little about a lot of things and speak judiciously about what they know. And finally, that rarity, the polymath who knows a great deal about everything. I have met only three such persons in my life.

One was the late Isaac Asimov, the second is Dr. Richard Long, Atticus Professor at Emory University in Georgia, and the third is Vusumsi Linda Make, a South African freedom fighter and onetime representative of the Pan African Congress, which was a volatile rival of the then conservative African National Congress.

The active mind replete with encyclopedic knowledge has always excited me, and when that brain is in the possession of a man, no matter what he looks like, I have found myself stirred physically and romantically.

When I was young and went frequently to public gatherings, I made certain to keep my ears and eyes alert for men of exceptional intelligence. Whenever I spotted such a man, my behavior was so uninhibited that women friends would admonish me in a stage whisper: "Maya, get to know him first."

John and Grace Killens gave a party for two South African freedom fighters who were at the UN to petition that world body to press for an end to apartheid. When I heard Vus Make's soft voice, filtering through its Xhosa accent, I perked up and leaned in toward him. He spoke to the entire gathering, but so far as I was concerned, he was talking just to me. He dazzled me with data and fractured me with facts. I sat erect, the very picture of rapt interest. Afterward he escorted me home. Two weeks later he proposed, and four weeks after we met we were honeymooning in London. Six months later I was questioning not only my judgment but my sanity.

True, he possessed every bit of information about the known world, how many square miles were arable in the Sahel, why the French were involved in Algeria's Black Hand organization, how long King Chaka had occupied the Zulu throne, how long Sisyphus had been pushing the rock, even how long the train has been gone, but he had no idea of how to make me happy. The same brain that retained reams of information, stacks of names, figures and dates, could not (I dare not think would not) deduce that I needed bedroom discourse, not boardroom dialogue, that our marriage was suffocating in the thin intellectual air that he breathed comfortably but that could not fill my lungs.

Because he was tender, I thought he was offering tenderness. He had startling intellect and an impressive accumulation of information, but was shy a mile from romance.

I left the marriage after it became lifeless, and I'm still thankful for the early passion we both brought to the union. I am even more thankful for the lesson learned. Heed the African saying "Be wary when a naked person offers you his shirt."

Poetic
Passage

*B*efore beginning a long and arduous journey the prudent traveler checks her maps, clocks and address-book entries and makes certain that her clothes will suit the weather she plans to encounter. If the trip includes crossing national boundaries, she examines her travel documents for their validity and, to the best of her ability, furnishes her wallet with the appropriate currency for her destination. This traveler urges us toward sober deliberation and stolid concentration. The second traveler is less careful, not so meticulous in planning the trip and, as a result, will encounter delays, disruptions and even despair. When disappointments mount to intolerable proportions, this traveler may even give up and return home, defeated. We learn from this example to either prepare well or stay at home.

It is the third, the desperate traveler, who teaches us the most profound lesson and affords us the most exquisite thrills. She touches us with her boldness and vulnerability, for her sole preparation is the fierce determination to leave wherever she is and her only certain destination is somewhere other than where she has been. An old blues describes this eager traveler:

I got the key to the Highway,
Booked down and I'm bound to go
I'm going to leave here running
'cause walkings most too slow.

Oprah Winfrey belongs to the third group of wanderers. She has been in voluntary transit since entering her teens. We know some sparse details of Oprah's passage, and stand in wonder at the awful inheritance that she had to either carry with her or jettison:

She was born poor and powerless in a land where
power is money and money is adored.

Born black in a land where might is white
and white is adored.

Born female in a land where decisions are masculine
and masculinity controls.

With such burdensome baggage it would seem that travel was unlikely if not downright impossible. Yet, among the red-clay hills of Mississippi the small, plain black girl with the funny name decided that she would travel and she would be her own conductor and porter. She would make the journey and carry her own baggage.

Today, even in the triumphal atmosphere that surrounds her, the keen observer can detect a steely determination in her voice and the resoluteness in her dark eyes.

She used faith, fate and a smile whose whiteness rivals a flag of truce to bring her from the dirt roads of the South to the world's attention. The Creator's blessings—intelligence, lively imagination and a relentless drive—have brought Oprah from the poignancy of a lonely childhood to the devotion of millions.

One loyal fan has said, "We can thank Oprah for some of the sanity in our country. She is America's most accessible and honest psychiatrist."

Oprah, as talk-show host, tries to maintain a calm façade as she lends an ear to brutes, bigots and bagmen, but her face often betrays her. Her eyes will fill with tears when she listens to the lament of mothers mistreated by their offspring, and they dart indignantly at the report of cruelty against children and savagery against the handicapped. The full lips spread into a wide, open smile when a guest or audience member reveals a daring spirit or a benevolent wit.

She is everyone's largehearted would-be sister who goes where the fearful will not tread. She asks our questions and waits with us for the answers.

The road has been long and the path has been stony. After her parents separated from each other and from her, she was left in the care of a grandmother who believed in the laying on of hands in all ways. She learned behavior from her grandmother, which she still honors today. She kneels nightly to thank God for His protection and generosity, for His guidance and forgiveness. She has a genuine fear of sin and sincerely delights in goodness. Unheralded success has not robbed her of her sense of wonder, nor have possessions made her a slave to property.

The little-girl laughter that erupts unexpectedly midsentence should not lure any observer into believing her to be childish, nor should the direct glance encourage any to feel that she is a hardened sophisticate. She is an honest, hardworking woman who has developed an unusual degree of empathy and courage. Oprah is making her journey at what might seem to be a dizzying pace, but it is her pace and she alone has set her tempo.

Art in
Africa

*A*frica, as impression, as idea, lies deep in the labyrinth of human imagination. Often its shape is beyond the will of words and its silhouette below the strata of conscious recovery. It lives in us on a primordial level, inexplicable but undeniable. We are the spring boughs with only the vaguest memory of winter's ruthless treatment of the tree. Despite a spate of nature documentaries, and despite endless shelves of travel books, Africa remains for most of us a hazy and remote illusion.

True or contrived, or possibly both true and contrived, African myths have wandered around the globe, half understood, half believed, half unbelievable, always adding to their mystery.

The unending human quest in Africa for treasure—that wild impulse toward the accumulation of precious metals, minerals and possession even of other human beings—can account for some of the misconceptions about Africa and the erroneous fantastic descriptions of the place and its peoples.

People could plow the earth with impunity for its bright gold and its glint of diamonds without determining that those wonderful elements were free booty only because they were found on "the dark continent."

The place of origin of Homo sapiens could not possibly have been stripped of its strongest sons and daughters for the purpose of satisfying greed unless one could name the place (and think of it) as not the First, or even Second, but the Third World.

The movements of the human tribe are traceable through the folktales, songs, detritus left by wars and the triumphal display of enemy totems captured by the victors, and it is possible to follow demographic shifts of families, clans and tribes by assessing their search for food, water, safety and arable land. We might conclude, then, that basic human need impels the species toward self-improvement as well as self-preservation. But an irresistible need to define oneself and a curiosity about the intangible nature of nature might just as logically explain why groups of nomadic human beings elect to stay in semipermanent homelands. And their art, the graphic descriptions of the known and the unknown, might have furnished the needed security in a world rife with insecurity.

For millennia, men have described their own masculine worlds, worlds both tangible and spiritual. They have used wood, bronze, stone and ivory. Their concepts of their universe gave shape to martial dances and substance to tales of battles ending in triumph or defeat. The unnamed sun and uncounted stars were given character and place in their stories. The tides and seasons were recognized by the rhythms of the men's drums.

In Africa, as in other places of the world, women created their own portraits—distinctive portraits of themselves and their universe. They used cloth, beads, leather and clay to express their views of the real and abstract worlds. Beliefs, spirits, omens, djinns, disappointments, fears and accomplishments were named, confessed, called, admitted and explained in the women's designs.

Their art, like all art, means to delight the eye, console the troubled mind, appease the highest authority and educate the children in the ways of the world. The aim also, whether or not articulated, is to infuse and sustain the family in an appreciation for life and the expectation of beauty.

West African women, unlike their East African sisters, eschew the bright reds and other primary colors. They allow themselves black, white, ocher, yellow and beige earth tones. They do employ blue, but it is the blue-black, electric indigo or the soft, subtle blue of West African mornings.

The Yoruba, one of West Africa's most ancient and surviving cultures, has roots extending back to 300 B.C. They were and are an artistically advanced people whose ancient symbols and mythologies are still in popular use and still influential. There is a Yoruba legend that explains the creation of the universe, Ife (the Yoruba Homeland) and human beings. The folktale praises Olakun, the goddess of the seas, as being an expert weaver. She is also reputed to possess an outstanding talent in the dyeing of cloth. In an attempt to regain her power over the earth, which was taken away from her because she acted rashly, Olakun challenges Olorun, the ruler of the sky, to a weaving contest. Olorun is aware of the power of her art and will not meet Olakun fairly. He sends a chameleon, which is able to instantly imitate all the goddess's colors and patterns. She concludes that if a lowly chameleon, who is only in the service of Olorun, is able to hold his own against her talents, then assuredly Olorun himself would defeat her. Thus, the woman's art of design and dyeing was never really bested or even matched by man. She was merely taken in by man's trickery, and her balance of art was set askew because she lost her internal moral balance.

Among most West African societies, outer beauty is believed to be the result of good inner moral character. The Yoruba love of moderation is expressed in their admiration of the cool character Iwu Tutu, which implies self-discipline, reflection and restraint.

The West African women's dress designs and patterns are said to set the continent's standard for modern modes, and are often found transformed in Western magazines of high fashion. Most of the ancient designs, whether on cloth, walls of houses or on earthenware, were inspired by proverbs and sayings. Today in some cases the meanings have been lost. But the illustrations have remained.

One popular West African design displays two and three rectangular forms crisscrossing on contrasting colored cloth. It is called Lai Momo, which translates from the Ga as Burnt Sticks. It comes from the saying "Wood once burned and allowed to go out will be more easily ignited than green wood, freshly hewn." When a woman attends a meeting of mediation, wearing Lai Momo, she tells the gathering that she is more amenable to reconciliation than to continuing the strife. So, as in all African life, art functions.

Another proverb that provided inspiration for a Nigerian cloth design is "If you do not appreciate the things you have, other people will treat them with contempt." Good counsel for both the young and the aged.

Whether or not the arrangement of lines and colors has remembered roots in ancient maxims, there is a great aesthetic sense that animates the crafts of painting, weaving, dyeing cloth and pot making. Women, using ordinary clay found in riverbeds and employing their hands as paintbrushes, produce a powerful vehicle for visual pleasure. Their crafts are also public statements of their personal creeds.

The simple materials are forged into plastic designs that will be as temporary as the length of time between rainfalls, and with no lasting staying power against the insistent sun. These artists, however, do not seem to need promises of longevity, nor do they exhibit a craving for notice out of the ordinary. In fact, one of the most notable characteristics of house painting among West African women is the camaraderie found among women sharing the creation of design. Family members and those attached by friendship often join together in the industry of decoration. When they do, it is agreed that the principal owner will contribute the major design, but it is also expected that every woman will bring something of her own to add to the overall effect.

Thus art made by all can be enjoyed by all. The African saying is proved true: Sea never dry.

Vacationing

*A*fter creating the universe, all the stars, each grain of sand, the humpback whale and the soft-shell crab, even God tired and took a day off.

There's no argument that we humans, who at our best can only create opportunities and at our worst create havoc, need time to rest.

I am not suggesting that vacations are a sacred right on a par with the right to vote, hold political office or to subscribe to one hundred magazines in order to compete for a $10 million lottery prize. No, I am merely observing that paltry creatures such as ourselves, who labor two-thirds of our lives to oppose gravity and remain erect, require some time to laze on sofas, relax before fireplaces, to recline on white beaches under a benevolent sun.

One would think those are not inordinate desires. We labor day and night to fill two small sacks in our chests with that which is everywhere available. We hold a torrent of blood inside our bodies, which are covered with tissue so thin that if we snag on a nail and do not close the aperture, the precious fluid would run out, leaving husks dry and lifeless.

All that is to say we work even when we are unaware of our efforts. So, we do need rest periods. However, there is that about us so perverse that even on a much-needed and hard-won holiday, we feel the irresistible need to spin and to toil.

On a beach in Mexico I sat near an artisan who had made some objects for sale. There were ash-colored birds, vases and other knickknacks, along with brushes in jars and bottles of paint.

I settled down comfortably, expecting to watch him turn the clay-colored objects into gay souvenirs. However, the man did not take up the brushes, nor did he touch the paint.

In moments a line formed before his table and buyers began to bargain. At each sale, the buyer was given a seat, which was taken eagerly. One woman noticed that I was watching. She smiled at me, a cat-with-bird-in-mouth smile.

"Here we get to paint them ourselves." Then I noticed the seller's sign, THINGS, HAND PAINTED.

I almost laughed aloud. These were tourists who had paid good money to come to Mexico to relax and here they were, working at something that if they had been asked to do, they would have declined without even thinking about it.

I was amazed at how they were squandering their free time, so what did I do? I rushed to my room, unpacked my yellow pads, got out my pen, dictionary and thesaurus, and sat down and took three days of my vacation to write this essay.

Age and
Sexuality

My husband was a man, my son a boy, so I accepted that it was my husband's right and responsibility to speak to our five-year-old son about sex. However, it didn't happen that way.

Guy came home from school one afternoon and asked me if I knew where babies come from. I admitted I did know. There was an "I bet you don't" look on his face and a "Got you this time" cockiness in his stance.

"Well, from where, then?" he asked.

This was not the moment to fudge or hesitate, and certainly not the time to say "Your father will tell you when he comes home."

I said, "Babies come from the mother's body."

He was crestfallen.

"How long have you known that?"

"For a long time."

"Well, why didn't somebody tell me?"

"I guess because you never asked before."

His interest seemed to ebb, and I offered him a glass of milk. I breathed deeply in relief as he drank.

He put the glass down on the counter and asked, "Do you know how the baby got in the mother's stomach?"

I had relaxed too soon. There was no slyness on his face. This time he was just a genuinely curious five-year-old. Again time had caught me in its clutch. I decided to be very matter-of-fact about the matter.

I reminded him of the names of his private parts. He nodded.

I said, "Well, when a couple wants a baby the man puts his penis into the woman's vagina and he deposits a sperm and the sperm meets the mother's egg and they grow together and after nine months the baby comes out."

Guy's face was scrambled into a mask of distaste. "Dad did that to you? Wow. You really must have wanted a baby bad."

"I wanted you."

"Wow. I'm glad you didn't want any more . . . or he'd be doing that all the time. Wow!"

Disgust took him out of the room, his small head wagging in puzzlement.

Alas, I have seen that same revulsion on children's faces when there is the slightest hint that their parents might be having sex. The extraordinary element in this account is that the children are in their thirties, forties and fifties.

An African American woman I know had parents who were married for forty years. The father had a lingering and painful illness during which the mother was his devoted and usually cheerful attendant. The father died. Three years later my acquaintance severed relations with her mother. The mother had dared to take up with a gentleman friend. The daughter, who is thirty-five years old and twice divorced, was repelled by the thought that her mother was being intimate with a man, and displeasure stretched beyond her control.

A group of friends and acquaintances met after church at a hotel for Sunday brunch. The unhappy woman let her horror over her mother's friend take control of the conversation.

"What could they possibly be doing together? She's nearly sixty and he's got to be sixty-five. Can you imagine them naked together? All that wrinkled skin rubbing against the other?"

Her face was an ugly mask. She puckered and pouted and sulked.

"Old people shouldn't have sex. Just thinking about that turns my stomach."

Sitting at the table were black women whose ages ranged from seventy to seventeen. There was silence for a moment after the tirade, then almost everyone began to speak at once.

"Are you crazy?"

"What's wrong with you?"

"Old folks don't have sex? Who told you that lie?"

One woman waited until the clamor had subsided and asked sweetly, "What do you think your momma and daddy did after you were born? They stopped doing the do?"

The whiner answered petulantly, "You don't have to be nasty." The statement brought howls of derision.

"Girl, you are sick."

"Get a grip."

And the oldest lady in the room said, "Honey, tired don't mean lazy, and every good-bye ain't gone."

I was reminded of my mother when she was seventy-four. She lived in California with my fourth stepfather, her great love, who was recovering from a mild stroke. Her telephone voice clearly told me how upset she was. "Baby. Baby, I've waited as long as I could before bothering you. But things have gone on too long. Much too long."

I made my voice as soft as hers had been hard. "Mom, what's the matter? I'll take care of it." Although I lived in North Carolina, I felt as close as the telephone, airlines and credit cards allowed me to be.

"It's your poppa. If you don't talk to him, I'm going to put his butt out. Out of this house. I'll put his butt on the street."

This last husband of Mom's was my favorite. We were made for each other. He had never had a daughter and I had not known a father's care, advice and protection since my teens.

"What did Poppa do, Mom? What is he doing?"

"Nothing. Nothing. That's it. He's not doing a damn thing."

"But, Mom, his stroke."

"I know. He thinks that if he has sex, he'll bring on another stroke. The doctor already told him that isn't true. And I got so mad when he said he might die having sex, that I told him there's no better way to go."

That was funny, but I knew better than to laugh.

"What can I do, Mom? Really, I mean there is nothing I can do."

"Yes, you can. You talk to him. He'll listen to you. Either you talk to him or I'll put him out on the street. I'm a woman, I'm not a damn rock."

I knew that voice very well. I knew that she had reached her level of frustration. She was ready to act.

I said, "OK, Mom. I don't know what I will say, but I'll talk to Poppa."

"You'd better do it soon, then."

"Mom, you leave the house at five-thirty this evening, and I'll telephone Poppa after you leave. Calm your heart, Mom, I'll do my best."

"OK, baby, 'bye. I'll talk to you tomorrow."

She was not happy, but at least she had calmed down. I pondered throughout the day and at six o'clock California time I telephoned.

"Hi, Poppa. How are you?"

"Hey, baby. How you doing?" He was happy to hear my voice.

"Fine, Poppa. Please let me speak to Mom."

"Oh, baby, she left here 'bout a half hour ago. Gone over to her cousin's."

"Well, Poppa, I'm worried about her and her appetite. She didn't eat today, did she?"

"Yes, she did. Cooked crab cakes and a slaw and asparagus. We ate it all."

"Well, she's not drinking, is she?"

"She had a beer with me, and you can bet she's got a Dewar's White Label in her hand right now."

"But, Poppa, something must be wrong. I mean, is she playing music and cards and things?"

"We played Take 6 all day on this music system you sent us, and I know she's playing dominoes over there with your cousin Mary."

"Well, Poppa, you seem to think her appetite is strong."

"Oh, yeah, baby, your momma got a good appetite."

"That's true, Poppa." I lowered my voice. "All her appetites are strong. Poppa, please excuse me—but

I'm the only one to speak to you—but it's true her love appetite is strong, too, and, Poppa, please excuse me, but if you don't take care of her in that department, she will starve to death, Poppa." I heard him cough, sputter and clear his throat.

"Please excuse me, Poppa, but someone is at my door. I love you, Poppa."

There was a very weak "Bye, baby."

My face was burning. I made a drink for myself. I had done the best I could, and I hoped it would work.

The next morning, about 7:00 A.M. California time, my mother's voice gave me the result.

"Hi, darling, Mother's baby. You are the sweetest girl in the world. Mother just adores you." She cooed and crooned, and I laughed for her pleasure.

Parents who tell their offspring that sex is an act performed only for procreation do everyone a serious disservice. With absolute distress, I must say that my mom died four years after that incident, but she remains my ideal. Now in my sixties, I plan to continue to be like her when I reach my seventies, and beyond, if I'm lucky.

Rural Museums— Southern Romance

*F*ast cars on four-lane highways and shiny crowded airports notwithstanding, there is a somnolent sense of literary connections in the state of Louisiana.

Along any late-night New Orleans street one might easily meet a Tennessee Williams character soliciting the kindness of strangers. Shreveport's old high houses, gabled and still, hold the other rooms and other places of Truman Capote's torturous childhood. Baton Rouge, eighty miles north of New Orleans, along Highway I-10, incongruously is Graham Greene country. When I went visiting the city, it was having its normal early-summer weather: steamy heat and the occasional shower that increased the humidity without lowering the feverish temperature.

I had come from my home in North Carolina to Baton Rouge to look at an outdoor folk museum that exhibits, among other things, slave cabins. Since I am a descendant of African slaves, my baggage was frightfully overweighted with trepidation, anger, fear and a morbid curiosity about the cabins. How did the slaves really live? How did they sleep after sunset and rise before daybreak? What and where did they eat? And, most crucially, I wondered if I would be able to survive this journey into my own hellish history.

The first inkling that I was traveling in a Graham Greene convoy in search of a character came when I talked with a bell captain at my hotel. Neat and proud of his efficiency, the young black man deposited my luggage, hung up the light bag, turned on lamps, tested the television and brought a bucket of ice.

I asked him, "How far are we from the Rural Life Museum?"

His face went blank as he turned the question over in his mind and chewed it on his lips. "The Rural Life Museum? Rural Life Museum . . ."

I said, "I was told it was quite near this hotel."

He reiterated, "The Rural Life Museum." He shook his head and almost immediately made what must have been for him a typically decisive gesture. "I'll find out, madam."

Later in the lobby he handed me a hotel pad. On the first page, written in decisive script, were clear directions to the location only five minutes away by car.

"Did you know that there are restored slave cabins on the place?" I asked.

His face again went blank, but this time there was no interest in the subject. "Slave cabins? Well, I'm sure you'll find them if you follow those directions, madam."

The boundaries of his world had been drawn so recently, were so modern and personal, that so far as he was consciously concerned, slavery and the Civil War, the invention of the cotton gin and the advent of talking pictures were equally sterile history.

Following the instruction "Turn first right after the exit," I passed the museum at first because the little gate looked like an entrance to a private residence. I succeeded on my second attempt and was rewarded with a 1.2-mile drive through the agricultural research experiment station given to Louisiana State University by Steele Burden and Miss Ione Burden. It is possible that I came between seasons, but the farms that yawned into the distance on either side of the road lay like abandoned Christmas wrappings after the precious contents had been removed.

I made myself imagine the plantation as it had been in the nineteenth century, when cotton was king and its favored subjects lived lives of exquisite luxury, while their minions existed under humiliating and painful circumstances. Looking out of my rental-car window, I placed the bent backs of five hundred slaves and saw the callused black fingers snatching desperately at the compliant white cotton. This was certainly

one aspect of the plantation character. Harry Bela-
fonte's voice came to me from a score of years earlier:

> *"You got to jump down*
> *turn around*
> *to pick a bale of cotton.*
> *Jump down*
> *turn around*
> *to pick a bale a day."*

I drove through the suffocating racial memories to
the entrance of the actual museum. There in a small
park all its own, surrounded by blooming flowers and
dark green ponds, was the bronze figure of *Uncle Jack.*
The sculpture is effective and telling. I once spent a
good part of a vacation admiring Michelangelo's
David in Florence. Despite diligent and constant ex-
amination, I am still not able to define where the
statue best exemplifies the truth of the human form.
Not in the legs alone, or the buttocks. Not in the
hard-muscled cylindrical neck, nor in the tapered fingers, dropping with natural ease. But it is the figure in
its entirety that renders the seldom-encountered realization of human physical perfection. Hans Schuller,
the sculptor of *Uncle Jack,* was also startlingly successful in realizing his intent. *Uncle Jack* is the quintessen-
tial obsequious Negro servant. His head is cocked to
the side and bowed deferentially. The droop of his

shoulders bears witness not only to his years but more specifically to his own understanding of his place as a poor black in a rich white world. His hand-me-down clothes, a few sizes too large, hang from his body with a sad finality. His right hand swings away from his body, appearing to offer the visitor a welcome greeting, but to me it seemed to say, You may have anything you see, me included.

I continued to the museum's office, housed in the barn. My reflections on the drive through the now sparsely attended farms had saddened me, but viewing the statue of Uncle Jack had wrought a great depression in my spirit. I paid the two-dollar entrance fee and carefully examined nineteenth-century surreys and sulkies that were being polished by a twentieth-century black man who I thought might well be a descendant of the slave who gave the carriages their first gloss. Still the figure of Uncle Jack imposed itself between the nineteenth-century vehicles and me.

The sculptor of *Uncle Jack* had employed the slavocracy's wishful romance that cast all blacks as congenitally subservient and only too happy to devote their lives to looking after their white folks. Neither the display of nineteenth-century farm implements nor a wooden slave collar fashioned to keep the slave confined but still ambulatory could erase my image of Uncle Jack caught for all time in his gruesome grin.

The rain was soft but persistent, and I, hatless, started for the slave cabins, but stopped at the overseer's house. That innocent-looking neat structure sat behind an equally innocent-looking and neat weathered fence and looked out upon the slave cabins with an avuncular if not paternal regard. The picture was so beneficent, I hurried over the water-soaked grass to the first cabin. Painted on the open door was a pretty and dignified black young woman standing protectively close to her small child. The interior of the abode revealed wooden chairs where the slave could go to rest after a day of honorable toil. There was also a colorfully blanketed bed, where he could stretch comfortably through a peaceful night until the bright morning.

At the museum I stood looking at the romance of slavery—gone were the humiliations and brutalities. But according to the narrative of Frederick Douglass, who escaped slavery in Maryland, slave quarters were little more than pigsties. Ten or more crowded together in hovels, often sleeping on packed-dirt floors. Winter and summer weather had their way in the cabins. Children were often fed at troughs like hogs. Here in this modern rendering of the past there was no evidence of the dread that slave families felt at the prospect of separation, nor the weariness of lives lived under the bludgeonings of a violent society. In the imagined old world created at Louisiana State University's Rural Life Museum, a group of assenting adults those centuries ago had worked the land in co-operative spirit for the common good.

I spent two days talking to local people "born an' bred in Batten Ruidge," who had never heard of the museum. I spoke to Steele Burden, who is the founder of the museum and donor of more than one thousand artifacts. He graciously gave me one of the Negro caricatures he makes. I politely refused a proffered group of black men shooting craps and accepted a small figure of a sugarcane worker.

On this journey in search of the character of a folk museum, I was reminded that ignorance is not genetic. A lack of courage allows us to remain blinded to our own history and deaf to the cries of our past. The museum is visited by thirty thousand people annually, and is used as a research facility for certain courses at the university. I could wish that professors and the fifty volunteers who act as guides would be bold enough to point out not only the architecture and artifacts but the salient missing factor: our historical truth.

I Dare
to Hope

*I*n 1992, as America's mighty marketing machines were being oiled and checked to begin selling and celebrating Christopher Columbus's feat of 1492, some people were reexamining with amazement and alarm another achievement that took place in Europe two decades after Columbus's lauded discovery. In the early 1500s Niccolò Machiavelli, exiled from his Italian home, wrote a slim manual on power, how to gain it, how to wield it and how to keep it. He named the handbook *The Prince* and dedicated it to Lorenzo de' Medici. The ideas therein so captured how to use what was base, weak and ignoble in the human psyche that for the past five hundred years when a person or action has been deemed devilish or satanically manipulative, it has been called Machiavellian. The advice he offered, which has been used so successfully against the powerless, can be paraphrased thus: Divide the masses that you may conquer them; separate them and you can rule them.

The staggering opposition to the nomination of

Clarence Thomas to the Supreme Court and its reams of media coverage sent me again to *The Prince.* I shook my head in sad disbelief over the present-day relevance and use of ideas summarized nearly five hundred years ago for the sole purpose of instructing the mighty on the management of the powerless.

The African American community whirled in eddies of debate, demolition, disagreement, accusation and calumny over the matter of whether an African American man with a lamentable reputation and impressive credentials should be seated on the highest court in the land. Thomas, chosen and appointed by President George Bush, demonstrated that he is as conservative as the president and the Bush administration. Otherwise he would not have been selected. The African American savants knew that, and knew as well that if efforts to scuttle his appointment were successful, another conservative possibly more detrimental to the cause of blacks and one who has neither history nor culture in common with us would be seated firmly on the bench till death ruled otherwise.

Thomas himself gave his adversaries every reason to oppose and distrust him. Many of his audacious actions as chairman of the Equal Employment Opportunity Commission were anti–affirmative action, anti-busing and anti other opportunities to redress inequality in our country.

In a federal district court case, as assistant secretary for civil rights, he allegedly testified that he had deliberately disobeyed a court order requiring the Department of Education to conduct speedy reviews of discrimination complaints. That admission, along with his indifference to African American issues, has given even his most staunch supporters pause.

Thomas, a poor black from Pinpoint, Georgia, reached proximity to America's highest court because of the very laws his forefathers fought to have written and enforced, and which he has treated so cavalierly.

It follows, then, that many African Americans ask, How can we advance if one we have sent forth in the vanguard ignores our concerns?

In these bloody days and frightful nights when an urban warrior can find no face more despicable than his own, no ammunition more deadly than self-hate and no target more deserving of his true aim than his brother, we must wonder how we came so late and lonely to this place. In this terrifying and murderous season, when young women achieve adulthood before puberty and become mothers before learning how to be daughters, we should stop the rhetoric and high-sounding phrases, stop the posing and preening and begin fiercely to look to our own welfare.

We need to haunt the halls of history and listen

anew to the ancestors' wisdom. We must ask questions and find answers that will help us to avoid dissolving into the merciless maw of history. How were our fore-fathers able to support their weakest when they them-selves were at their weakest? How were they able to surround the errant leader and prevent him from being coopted by forces that would destroy him and them? How were they—lonely, bought separately, sold apart—able to conceive of the deep wisdom found in the advice "Walk together, children . . . don't you get weary."

The black youngsters of today must ask black leaders, "If you can't make an effort to reach, recon-struct and save a black man who has been to and graduated from Yale, how can you reach down here in this drug-filled, hate-filled cesspool where I live and save me?"

I supported Clarence Thomas's nomination, and was neither naive enough nor hopeful enough to imagine that in publicly supporting him I gave the younger generation a pretty picture of unity. I wanted rather to show them that they and I come from a peo-ple who had the courage to exist, to be when being was dangerous, who had the courage to dare when daring was dangerous, and—most important—who had the courage to hope.

Because Clarence Thomas has been poor, has

been nearly suffocated by the acrid odor of racial discrimination, is intelligent, well trained, black and
young enough to be won over again, I supported him.

The prophet in Lamentations cried, "Although he
put his mouth in the dust . . . there is still hope."

Poor
Poverty

*H*ow poor were you?

We were so poor we thought the only thing edible about a chicken was its feet, about the cow its tail, about a hog its intestine and its ankles.

Such one-liners can amuse because the listener knows that the person who isn't aware of poverty is spared its most cruel lash. For it is hateful to be young, bright, ambitious and poor. The added insult is to be aware of one's poverty.

Before television brought pictures of luxurious living rooms and glistening kitchens into the view of the impoverished, they could pretend, tell themselves that only the few, the lucky, maybe just their employers, lived lives of refined comfort.

But today, when every soap opera is rife with characters whose great wealth is only equaled by their moral neediness, paupers watching in shacks on every street are forced to admit that they are indeed poverty-stricken.

With that knowledge and acknowledgment, there

comes inevitably a lingering despair and a puzzling wretchedness. Why them and not me? Those questions are followed by a sense of worthlessness—a remorseful regret at being alive. Then comes full-blown anger, resentment, a rankling bitterness that, if directed outward, can foment riots, revolution and social chaos. Most often, however, the convulsions of anger are directed inward. Thus the poor, the needy, the misfits of society implode. After the debris settles, they appear to the onlookers as dry husks of hopelessness.

If it is true that a chain is only as strong as its weakest link, isn't it also true a society is only as healthy as its sickest citizen and only as wealthy as its most deprived?

I believe so.

Danger in
Denial

*T*here has been a cacophony of sound, a screaming atonal symphony of noise in the African American community. Some serious thinkers and some ponderous prophets bemoan the chasm that exists between the sexes. The general consensus is that the rift is so wide and deep that it cannot be bridged. Hip-hop rappers prove the prognosis correct when they describe black women—their mothers, grandmothers, great-grandmothers and their current squeezes—as ho's, bitches and other menaces to the well-being of black men.

It is hard to comprehend how we have grown so far apart.

We were stolen and sold from the African continent together. We crouched together in the barracoons, without enough air to share between us. We lay, back to belly, in the filthy hatches of slave ships, in one another's excrement, menstrual blood and urine. We were hosed down and oiled to give sheen to our skin, then stood together on auction blocks and were sold together. We rose before sunrise from the cold ground, were driven into the cane field and the cotton field together. We each took the lash that pulled the skin from our backs. Each of us was singled out for the sexual enjoyment and exploitation of those who desired our bodies but hated us.

How have we come so quickly to forget the lessons we were forced to learn together?

Why have we subjugated our memory in the vain hope that we will be able to live above and beyond history? When will we cease presiding over the mutilation of memory?

I prefer the remembrance, the painful bitter recall. I know that I need a brother who shares this tender, taunting heritage. I desire a sister who is not in denial of our mutual past. Together, we may be able to plan a less painful future. Separate, we can only anticipate further ruptures and deeper loneliness.

The Rage
Against
Violence

Some months ago two beautiful, powerful and world-famous women sat in my dining room. They were remarking about the danger of our time, the random shootings, the stalkings and the general mayhem and murder in the streets.

They asked how I dealt with violence. I answered that my response was mostly to stay out of its way if possible, but if it is brought into my life, then I do my best to oust it from my presence as quickly as possible. When they asked for an example I told them a story that involved my petite mother when she was visiting me in New York. We were invited to a party on Long Island and our hosts sent a limousine to take us to the affair. We went to 151st and Riverside to collect a sister friend who was going to attend the party.

Years before, the building had been a gracious, stately edifice with fine rugs and antique furniture in the lobby. There had been a doorman who spoke English and welcomed visitors with a courtly air.

I didn't tell my mother that the once elegant

building had fallen prey to the drug madness and that the doorman had long since departed, and that since the front-door lock had been broken, all the former gracious appurtenances had disappeared.

When we arrived at the building my little mother put her hand on an equally small person, a white television producer who was sharing the ride. "You come with me," my mother said.

I said, "No, I'll go get her." My mother, whose voice was usually sweet and light, changed it into the rumble of a German tank and said, "You stay here—Al and I will go."

I watched their backs as they entered the dirty lobby, and felt as if I were watching innocent Christians entering a lion-filled arena in Nero's Rome.

I learned later that this is what happened: In the elevator Mother pressed the button for the sixth floor. The elevator immediately lurched downward. At the basement a man entered, unkempt and wild-eyed. He looked at my mother and the trembling white friend and asked, "How far are you going?" Mother picked up on the beat in a second: "I'm going all the way. I got in this elevator to go all the way. I mean all—the—way. How far are you going?" The man didn't answer but got off on the first floor. My mother and her friend continued to their floor.

· · ·

Somehow and for some vague and inane reason, we have decided it is better to be exploited, misused, battered and bedraggled than to become disagreeable. We think that possibly the brute, who is prepared to treat a victim in the most unkind way, will be coerced into being more kind if the victim is courteous. I don't agree. If I am attacked, when I have done nothing to warrant an attack, or even if I have, I work myself up into a fury much more explosive than the miscreant can imagine. I jump into a righteous lather. And I mean to make myself more to deal with than the brute can handle. I mean if I can make myself get mad before I get scared the evildoer will rue the day.

Art for
the Sake
of the Soul

miss rosie
when i watch you
wrapped up like garbage
sitting, surrounded by the smell
of too old potato peels
or
when i watch you
in your old man's shoes
with the little toe cut out
sitting, waiting for your mind
like next week's grocery
i say
when i watch you
you wet brown bag of a woman
who used to be
   (the best-looking gal in Georgia)
used to be called the Georgia Rose
i stand up
through your destruction
i stand up.

That poem was written by Lucille Clifton, an African American poet who teaches in universities all over the United States. It seems to me the perfect explanation of how we human beings have managed to stand erect—how, often brought to our knees by our own greed, chicanery or ignorance, we manage to pull ourselves up to a standing position.

Miss Clifton has suggested miss rosie, a beleaguered, battered and lonely old woman as her inspiration, and using the same poem, in each instance I insert the word "art," for "miss rosie," for I believe that art encourages us to stand erect and stretch upward toward the higher ground.

I believe that without the presence and energy of art in our lives, we are capable of engaging in heartless activities without remorse and cruelties with clear consciences. We become base because we think of ourselves only as base. We find no delight in immaterial things, and address ourselves and each other in the cruelest terms, for we believe we are deserving of nothing better.

I grew up in an Arkansas that seemed to me to be a place on no one's planet or, for that matter, on no one's mind. The relentless poverty of the Depression, allied with the virulent racial prejudices of the time, had the power to grind the spirit into submission and pulverize the very ability to dream. Yet, I, as well as others, survived those lean years and those mean Arkansas roads, and I think we survived particularly because of the inheritance of black American art, an inheritance left to us by our forebears as surely as steel magnates left massive fortunes for their heirs.

In Stamps, Arkansas, when parents on their way to the cotton fields left small children too young to work in the care of others too old to work, they knew that the baby tenders would recite Paul Laurence Dunbar's poems to their children. Thus, even if a father was twenty miles away, his son would know of his father's love for him because the older person would recite and act out:

> Little brown baby wif spa'klin' eyes,
>> Come to yo' pappy an' set on his knee.
> What you been doin', suh—
>>> makin' san' pies?
>> Look at dat bib—you's ez du'ty ez me.
> Look at dat mouf—dat's merlasses, I bet;
>> Come hyeah, Maria, an' wipe off his han's.
> Bees gwine to ketch you
>>> an' eat you up yit,
>> Bein' so sticky and sweet—goodness lan's!
> Little brown baby wif spa'klin' eyes,
>> Who's pappy's darlin'
>>> an' who's pappy's chile?

Who is it all de day nevah once tries
  Fu' to be cross, er once loses dat smile?
Whah did you git dem teef?
     My, you's a scamp!
Whah did dat dimple com f'om
    in yo' chin?
Pappy do' know you—
     I b'lieves you's a tramp;
  Mammy, dis hyeah's
     some ol' straggler got in!
Let's th'ow him outen de do' in de san',
  We do' want stragglers
     a-layin' 'roun' hyeah;
Let's gin him 'way to de big buggah-man
  I know he's hidin' erroun' hyeah
     right neah.
Buggah-man, buggah-man, come in de do',
  Hyeah's a bad boy you kin have fu' to eat.
Mammy an' pappy do' want him no mo',
  Swaller him down f'om his haid to his feet!
Dah, now, I t'ought dat you'd
    hug me up close.
  Go back, ol' buggah,
    you sha'nt have dis boy.
He ain't no tramp, ner no straggler,
    of co'se;
  He's pappy's pa'dner an' playmate
    an' joy.

Come to you' pallet now—go to yo' res';
Wisht you could allus know ease
                                    an' cleah skies
Wisht you could stay jes' a chile
                on my breas'—
Little brown baby wif spa'klin' eyes!

The strength of the black American to withstand the slings and arrows and lynch mobs and malignant neglect can be traced directly to the arts of literature, music, dance and philosophy that, despite significant attempts to eradicate them, remain in our communities today.

The first Africans were brought to this country in 1619. I do not mean to cast aspersions on my white brothers and sisters who take such pride in having descended from the Pilgrims, but I would remind them that the Africans landed in 1619, which was one year before the arrival of the *Mayflower*. We have experienced every indignity the sadistic mind of man could devise. We have been lynched and drowned and beleaguered and belittled and begrudged and befuddled. And yet, here we are. Still here. Here. Upward of forty million, and that's an underestimate. Some people swear there are more than forty million black people in the Baptist Church. They're not even including other denominations or backsliders or black atheists in the world. How, then, have we survived?

Because we create art and use our art immediately. We have even concealed ourselves and our pain in our art. Langston Hughes wrote:

Because my mouth
Is wide with laughter
And my throat
Is deep with song,
You do not think
I suffer after
I have held my pain
So long.

Because my mouth
Is wide with laughter
You do not hear
My inner cry
Because my feet
Are gay with dancing
You do not know
I die.

When a larger society would have us believe that we have made no contribution of consequence to the Western world—other than manual labor, of course—the healing, the sustaining and the supporting roles of art were alive and well in the black community.

An incident that occurred years ago informed me of the power of African American contributions. I was a member of the opera company performing *Porgy and Bess*. I was the first dancer, very young, blitheringly ignorant. I never called myself first dancer, but, rather, referred to myself as première danseuse or prima ballerina. I sang the role of Ruby, but I sang it by heart. I had trained as a dancer, not as a singer, but I had sung in church, and so I had learned to sing, somewhat. But I was no threat to the singers, of whom there were forty-five and who among themselves had 120 degrees in music. There were so few places for black singers trained in classical music to work that the company could afford to get a person who had one degree from Curtis and another from Juilliard just for the chorus.

We traveled throughout Europe and arrived in Morocco while the company sent the sets on to Spain. Black opera singers, white opera singers, Native American opera singers, Spanish-speaking opera singers, Aleut opera singers, Asian . . . all opera singers are one people, much like New York taxi drivers. They're all cut from the same cloth.

The singers were informed by the conductor that since the sets had been sent on to Spain, they were obliged to perform in a concert. They were ready. They had their portfolios, I am sure, on microfiche, jammed up in the heels of their shoes. They were ab-so-lutely ready.

I said to the conductor, "I'm sorry, I have no aria. That is not my field." He was Russian with masses of Russian artistic temperament. He fell back two whole steps and clutched his hair and said in a heavy Russian accent, "But don't you at least know one spiritual?"

I didn't say this to him, but I thought to myself, Is grits groceries? Do I know a spiritual? I grew up in church. Sunday, all day, and every evening of the week found me and my family in church, and at all those gatherings we sang. So, of course I could sing a spiritual. I looked at him and said, "I will try to think of something."

The other singers went out that evening and delivered beautifully the important arias in the canon of European classical music, and they were very well received. Near the end of the concert the conductor beckoned me onto the stage.

I thought of a song my grandmother sang in that little town in Arkansas. Every Sunday for ten years, I had gone through the same ritual: We would gather in church. Fifteen minutes after the service began the preacher would say, "And now we'll be privileged with a song from Sister Henderson." Each Sunday, my grandmother would respond, "Me?" Then she would take her time, look up at the ceiling as if she was considering: What on earth could I possibly sing? And every Sunday she sang the same song.

In Morocco, all alone on the stage, I sang her song:

I'm a poor pilgrim of sorrow.
I'm lost in this wide world alone.

I sang the whole song through, and when I finished, forty-five hundred Arabs jumped up, hit the floor and started to shout. I was young and ignorant. I had no idea of the power of this, my inherited art. I didn't know what to do. I looked stage right and stage left at the singers who had always treated me as if I were a mascot because I offered them no competition as a singer. Every night, one or another of them would come out and almost pat my head and say, "Maya, sorry to tell you, you flatted the E," or "Oh, Maya, mmmm, you sharped that G!"

But I looked at them now. I looked stage left and stage right, where they were crowded together glowering at me. I said, "I'm sorry. I'm sorry. I'm sorry that I have the glory . . ." They had sung Respighi, Rossini, Bach, Bloch, Beethoven, lovely lieder and lovely Britten art songs, and they had been well received. And I had sung what Dr. Du Bois called a sorrow song, not written by the free and easy, not written by anyone credited with being creative, and forty-five hundred people had leaped into the palm of my hand.

"Why?" I walked alone that night in Morocco, my first time in North Africa. I thought, Oh, it's because they feel sorry for the poignancy of my slave history. I later learned that the people in the audience had no idea of my slave history. Why, then?

Great art belongs to all people, all the time—indeed it is made for the people by the people.

I have written of the black American experience, which I know intimately. I am always talking about the human condition in general and about society in particular. What it is like to be human, and American, what makes us weep, what makes us fall and stumble and somehow rise and go on from darkness into darkness—that darkness carpeted with figures of fear and the hounds behind and the hunters behind and one more river to cross, and oh, my God, will I ever reach that somewhere, that safe getting-up morning. I submit to you that it is art that allows us to stand erect.

In that little town in Arkansas, whenever my grandmother saw me reading poetry she would say, "Sister, Mama loves to see you read the poetry because that will put starch in your backbone." When people who were enslaved, whose wrists were bound and whose ankles were tied, sang,

> *I'm gonna run on,*
> *See what the end is gonna be . . .*

I'm gonna run on,
See what the end is gonna be . . .

the singer and the audience were made to understand that, however we had arrived here, under whatever bludgeoning of chance, we were the stuff out of which nations and dreams were made and that we had come here to stay.

I'm gonna run on,
See what the end is gonna be . . .

Had the blues been censored, we might have had no way of knowing that our looks were not only acceptable but even desirable. The larger society informed us all the time—and still does—that its idea of beauty can be contained in the cruel, limiting, ignorant and still current statement that suggests you can't be too thin, or too rich, or too white. But we had the nineteenth-century blues in which a black man informed us, talking about the woman that he loved,

The woman I love is fat
And chocolate to the bone,
And every time she shakes,
Some skinny woman loses her home.

Some white people actually stand looking out of windows at serious snow falling like cotton rain, covering the tops of cars and streets and fire hydrants and say, "My God, it sure is a black day."

So black people had to find ways in which to assert their own beauty. In this song the black woman sang:

> *He's blacker than midnight,*
> *Teeth like flags of truth.*
>
> *He's the finest thing in the whole St. Louis.*
> *They say the blacker the berry,*
> *Sweeter is the juice. . . .*

That is living art, created to encourage people to hang on, stand up, forbear, continue.

I suggest that we must be suspicious of censors who say they mean to prohibit our art for our own welfare. I suggest that we have to question their motives and tend assiduously to our own personal and national health and our general welfare. We must replace fear and chauvinism, hate, timidity and apathy, which flow in our national spinal column, with courage, sensitivity, perseverance and, I even dare say, "love." And by "love" I mean that condition in the human spirit so profound it encourages us to develop courage. It is said that courage is the most important of all the virtues, because without courage you can't practice any other virtue with consistency.

We must infuse our lives with art. Our national leaders must be informed that we want them to use our taxes to support street theater in order to oppose street gangs. We should have a well-supported regional theater in order to oppose regionalism and differences that keep us apart. We need nationally to support small, medium and large art museums that show us images of ourselves, those we like and those we dislike. In some way that is very important to us we need to see those we dislike even more than those we like because somehow we need at least glancing visions of how we look "as in a mirror darkly."

Our singers, composers and musicians must be encouraged to sing the song of struggle, the song of resistance, resistance to degradation, resistance to our humiliation, resistance to the eradication of all our values that would keep us going as a country. Our actors and sculptors and painters and writers and poets must be made to know that we appreciate them, that in fact it is their work that puts starch in our backbones.

We need art to live fully and to grow healthy. Without it we are dry husks drifting aimlessly on every ill wind, our futures are without promise and our present without grace.

Those Who
Really Know
Teach

*T*hey don't know beans. Not even beans about beans." Vivian's face wrinkled with pity, anger and disgust. "Didn't they have mothers? Aunties? Grandmothers? Were they raised in barns?"

She didn't attempt to lower her voice, and I knew it was useless to try to interest her in another area of the supermarket. Near the butcher's counter, where we were standing, the dark, cold air smelled of old blood.

"Here it is, payday. She's got her or her man's check, and she's buying two T-bone steaks and a few pounds of hamburger, and the Lord knows what's ground up in that mess."

A young black woman who was the target of my mother's tirade looked up and, raking us with a withering stare, abruptly turned her back. I could have hugged her. I understood her reaction completely.

Older black women can scrape the skin from one's body by the artful use of particular words and a certain cadence in the speech. The process is called signifying, and has an African origin. Since the victim of the tirade is never spoken to directly or called by a name, there is no rejoinder possible except to roll one's eyes, purse one's lips and shrug the shoulders in a way to suggest Shoo fly, don't bother me.

"That's why I want to open a cooking school— she could be my first student. I would show her that it's better to buy a whole roast, cut it into steaks and sprinkle that meat with tenderizer and garlic powder. Huh, she'd save money and have food so good her husband would want to go to work on Sunday." Mother directed her speech to me, but I watched the woman and caught her smiling.

"I could show her how to turn turkey wings into a dish so good it would make a rabbit hug a hound and make a preacher lay his Bible down."

The woman turned, looked at my mother and grinned broadly. She said, "Well, I sure want to know how to do that."

My mother had the gall to look surprised. "I beg your pardon." The woman said nothing, but continued smiling. Mother said, "Oh, you must have overheard me talking to my daughter. This is my daughter, Maya. What's your name?"

"Ophelia." She offered her hand. "Yes, ma'am, I heard you talking about steak and turkey wings. I love turkey, but I've never learned how to cook turkey wings."

Mother was still holding the woman's hand when she turned to me. "Baby, you get the sausage and a nice plump roaster. I'm going to buy this young woman a cup of coffee over at that counter."

She smiled at me, at the woman, at the world and at life, and said, "Come on, Ophelia, I'm going to tell you some home truths."

I watched as Ophelia trailed after my mother, who was still holding her hand.

Many people are graduated from teacher-training academies, but one has to have a calling to become a true teacher. And above all things, one needs a bounty of courage.

The calling informs the teacher that her knowledge is needed in new uncharted areas, and the courage makes the teacher dare the journey. My mother had both.

Even
the Stars
Look Lonesome
Sometimes

During the sixties an acquaintance of mine left her home in Mississippi. Left her family and church and social groups. Left her choir and suitors, assured by her uncommon good looks that she would find the truly high life in the big city.

She moved to Chicago, found a menial job and a very small room. To her dismay, no one took particular notice of her, because there were prettier girls who were also wittier and who dressed more smartly.

Instead of trying to re-create the ambiance she had left, instead of trying to build a circle of family friends, instead of trying to find a church and join the choir, she went to singles bars, and with a sad desperation searched and found company that she would take back to her pitiful room and keep overnight at any cost.

I met her at a Chicago club where she was a regular. I had a two-week contract to sing at Mr. Kelly's, and despite my debut nerves, I noticed her on the first night.

Her clothes were too tight, her makeup too heavy, and she clapped too loudly, laughed too often, and there was a pathetic eagerness hanging about her. We met on the third night, and on the fourth night she told me her story. It sobered and saddened me. I asked why she didn't go home. She said her relatives had died and no one else in town wanted her.

In the biblical story, the prodigal son risked and for a time lost everything he had because of an uncontrollable hunger for company. First, he asked for and received his inheritance, not caring that his father, from whom he would normally inherit, was still alive; not considering that by demanding his portion, he might be endangering the family's financial position. The parable relates that after he took his fortune, he went off into a far country and there he found company. Wasteful living conquered his loneliness and riotous companions conquered his restlessness. For a while he was fulfilled, but he lost favor in the eyes of his friends. As his money began to disappear he began to slip down that steep road to social oblivion.

His condition became so reduced that he began to have to feed the hogs. Then it further worsened until he began to eat with the hogs. It is never lonesome in Babylon. Of course, one needs to examine who—or in the prodigal son's case, what—he has for company. Many people remind me of the journey of the prodigal son. Many believe that they need company at any cost, and certainly if a thing is desired at any cost, it will be obtained at all costs.

We need to remember and to teach our children that solitude can be a much-to-be-desired condition. Not only is it acceptable to be alone, at times it is positively to be wished for.

It is in the interludes between being in company that we talk to ourselves. In the silence we listen to ourselves. Then we ask questions of ourselves. We describe ourselves to ourselves, and in the quietude we may even hear the voice of God.

ABOUT THE AUTHOR

MAYA ANGELOU, author of the bestselling *Even the Stars Look Lonesome, I Know Why the Caged Bird Sings, Gather Together in My Name, Singin' and Swingin' and Gettin' Merry Like Christmas, Wouldn't Take Nothing for My Journey Now* and the Oprah Book Club selection *The Heart of a Woman*, has also written five collections of poetry: *Just Give Me a Cool Drink of Water 'fore I Diiie; Oh Pray My Wings Are Gonna Fit Me Well; And Still I Rise; Shaker, Why Don't You Sing?* and *I Shall Not Be Moved*, as well as *On the Pulse of Morning*, which was read by her at the inauguration of President William Jefferson Clinton on January 20, 1993. In theater, she produced, directed and starred in *Cabaret for Freedom* in collaboration with Godfrey Cambridge at New York's Village Gate, starred in Genet's *The Blacks* at the St. Mark's Playhouse and adapted Sophocles' *Ajax*, which premiered at the Mark Taper Forum in Los Angeles in 1974. In film and television, she wrote the original screenplay and musical score for the film *Georgia, Georgia* and wrote and produced a ten-part TV series on African traditions in American life. In the sixties, at the request of Dr. Martin Luther King, Jr., she became Northern coordinator for the Southern Christian Leadership Conference, and in 1975 she received the *Ladies' Home Journal* Woman of the Year Award in communications. She has received numerous honorary degrees, was appointed by President Jimmy Carter to the National Commission on the Observance of International Women's Year and by President Gerald R. Ford to the American Revolution Bicentennial Advisory Council. She is on the board of trustees of the American Film Institute. One of the few female members of the Directors Guild, Angelou is the author of the television screenplays *I Know Why the Caged Bird Sings* and *The Sisters*. Most recently, she wrote lyrics for the musical *King: Drum Major for Love* and was both host and writer for the series of documentaries *Maya Angelou's America: A Journey of the Heart,* along with Guy Johnson. Angelou is currently Reynolds Professor at Wake Forest University, Winston-Salem, North Carolina.